THE MINDSET AND HABITS OF

SUCCESSFUL

ENTREPRENEURS

by

SEAN MCCAFFERY

Contents

Introduction

"Achievement seems to be connected with action. Successful men and women keep moving. They make mistakes but they don't quit."

- Conrad Hilton

Each of us has our own unique definition of success. For some, it might be working from home and enjoying a consistent stream of income. For others, it might translate to an enormous amount of wealth or even celebrity. For still others, success may just mean seeing something through to completion or gaining a sense of peace.

While there are so many ways we think of success, there are just as many variations on the notion of the *successful entrepreneur*.

After all, you may start a business with a non-profit mission, focusing more on empowering people rather than earnings; another person might become the successful owner of an online business that is all about monetizing their activities and endeavors.

Where both examples are alike, though, is in their achievement, their successes. Clearly, there must be something at work driving successful entrepreneurs, some sort of similar set of skills or habits, right?

Interestingly enough, it is what lies beneath success where you find the answer. And what lies beneath? It is a particular kind of *mindset* that seems to drive people from all different backgrounds, and with differing philosophies and goals, towards entrepreneurial success.

While you can read countless handbooks on the work ethics, patterns or behaviors of the world's biggest entrepreneurs, or articles on "how to succeed in business or life", it has to all begin with your mindset.

This book has been titled *"The Mindset & Habits of Successful Entrepreneurs"* and we need you to pay attention to that word order. First, we are going to focus on mindset, and then habits.

First, Mindset

Mindset is the key, especially what is known in psychological circles as the "growth mindset". This is a way of thinking, knowing, believing and behaving that is entirely opposite of what psychologists call the "fixed mindset". In the chapters that follow, we'll learn the differences between them, and then discover how the growth mindset is such a serious advantage for those who develop it.

Not only will it help you to commit and persevere in the development of winning habits, but it is also the way of thinking that allows you to overcome obstacles, build your character, broaden your skill set, expand your intellect and accept that success does not come from good luck or inherited talents. It comes from what you see as possible versus what you refuse to see as achievable.

Your mindset is what gets you out of bed, steers you towards the most productive steps or actions, allows you to focus, and even tells you to take the road less travelled or the more challenging path because that will lead you to success - even it begins with failures.

Then, Entrepreneurial Habits

Now, entrepreneurs, according to Forbes are "those who identify a need--- any need--- and fill it. It's a primordial urge, independent of product, service, industry or market." In a 2012, article, the site even described entrepreneurs as the "seek and solve breed". This is actually in perfect alignment with the growth mindset, always eager to problem solve, grow and improve.

Forbes also claimed that "the true essence of entrepreneurship [is to] Define, invest, build, repeat." You cannot do that if you see yourself as limited or required to be flawless in your performance of specific tasks, but that is what happens with the fixed mindset.

It is the growth mindset of all successful entrepreneurs that allows them to believe it is possible, but only if they learn and commit to doing what it takes to make it happen.

And what do you need to do to make it happen? Developing specific habits will ensure you are persistently moving towards success. Is it your habit to remain open to suggestions or do you dismiss anything recommended by a colleague or client as criticism? Do you work, constantly, on communication methods or use a stock array of approaches? Habits are not just about simple issues like how you dress or what sort of routine you follow, and they are the other half of the equation where entrepreneurial success is concerned.

But first, that mindset. ..Not sure you have that kind of mindset? The good news is that formal studies have proven you can develop it, and then use it in your own successful entrepreneurial pursuits. If you are ready to develop a growth mindset and develop the habits of successful entrepreneurs, let's begin!

Chapter One

Mindset

"I'm convinced that about half of what separates the successful entrepreneurs from the non-successful ones is pure perseverance."

- Steve Jobs

A Mindset Check

If you aim at becoming a successful entrepreneur, it is important to have more than a "can do" attitude or some clearly laid out plans for your business venture. While there is no doubt that such factors are going to help you reach goals, there is a more important component - your mindset.

According to Inc., it is a "particular and profoundly powerful mindset" needed to drive your success. Of course, we need to know what "mindset" really means...

Mindset Defined

Mindset is a term we might use to describe something like our mood or attitude, but it is far more than that. Psychology Today defines it as "a belief that orients the way we handle situations — the way we sort out what is going on and what we should do. Our mindsets help us spot opportunities but they can trap us in self-defeating cycles."

As author Carol Dweck writes, "the view you adopt for yourself profoundly affects the way you lead your life. It can determine whether you become the person you want to be and whether you commit to and accomplish the things you value."

In other words, your mindset is a lot like your world view, and it encompasses your view of yourself. It shapes your beliefs and in doing that, it creates a framework for how you view, handle, see or achieve anything in life. As experts warn, though, it can be selfdefeating as much as it can be helpful.

So as a very savvy first step towards success, we are going to determine what sort of mindset *you have now*, and learn if you might be already sabotaging yourself, or alternately, heading right into success, through your mindset.

Growth v. Fixed

As we discussed in the Introduction, psychologists and behavioral experts accept that we might have a *fixed* or a *growth* mindset.

The fixed mindset is one in which you thoroughly and whole heartedly believe that your abilities and skills are fixed, unchangeable and simply "the hand you were dealt". As Dweck writes, "People with a fixed mindset believe that their traits are just givens. They have a certain amount of brains and talent and nothing can change that. If they have a lot, they're all set, but if they don't..."

This is that self-defeating cycle that Psychology Today warned of, it would include the belief that you don't have the natural talent or intelligence to excel at something. And somewhat surprisingly, the fixed mindset typically insists on perfection and excellence at what it recognizes as your existing skill or talent.

It is never enough to succeed at the basic level, the fixed mindset becomes, well... fixated on attaining a level of flawlessness in whatever talents or skills are present, and that leads to constant setbacks and failures. As Dweck says, "this mindset gives you no good recipe for overcoming it. If failure means you lack competence or potential—that you are a failure - where do you go from there?"

As a simple example, a person with a fixed mindset might come up with a great idea. They spend time hashing out some of the basic concepts, and then start looking around the Internet to see if others are already doing this business or enterprise. Upon discovering some sites showing others already succeeding, and with deeper backgrounds in the industry, the person with the fixed mindset might feel their lack of experience, skills and education will make it impossible for them to compete. They have already chosen to fail because they cannot be a top performer or go to it without risk of failure or of looking less qualified than others.

The person with the growth mindset would be unable to resign themselves to such a status.

The growth mindset is defined as one in which an individual views their personal qualities or traits as things they can enhance or develop if they are dedicated and hard working.

They can be people already gifted with specific talents, but the individual with the growth mindset thinks of their gifts or talents as a foundation or starting point. They realize that Mozart would not have become Mozart if he didn't practice passionately and learn more and more about music as he grew in skill and mastery, or that Tiger Woods would not have reached such enormous success without constant practice and commitment.

Now, don't get this wrong - the person with the fixed mindset does not believe that all people can turn into Einsteins or that they themselves can be trained or educated into being the next Tom Brady.

No, what they believe is quite simple: they see that their potential (or anyone's potential) as an unknown, and accept that it is impossible to guess or know what that potential will become with many years of training, work and dedication.

So, if we go back to that earlier example and see an entrepreneur with a good idea for a business, we would see them do the research, see what it takes to get from point A to point Z and dig in. They would examine the "what if" scenarios, look for that niche to fill, and do as we stated earlier: define, invest, build and repeat; and would do so until they succeeded.

Which is Your Mindset?

So, which mindset do you feel you currently have? It is easy enough to find an answer. Consider the following questions, giving a yes or no answer to each, and being entirely honest along the way:

1. We each have a certain amount of intelligence, and can't do anything to change it.

2. Our intelligence is something that cannot be changed very much.

3. Honestly, we can't change our level of intelligence.

4. We can learn new things, but can't really change our level intelligence

5. Sincerely, we can't really change how much talent we have.

6. We have a certain amount of talent, and can't really do much to change it.

7. Our talent in any given area is something that can't change very much.

8. We can learn new things, but can't really change our basic level of talent.

9. We can always substantially change how intelligent we are.

10. No matter how much intelligence we have, we can always change it quite a bit.

11. We can change even our basic level of intelligence significantly.

12. Regardless of who you are, you can change your intelligence level significantly

13. No matter who we are, we can significantly change our level of talent.

14. We can always change how much talent we have substantially.

15. No matter how much talent we have, we can always change it quite a bit.

16. We can considerably change even our basic level of talent.

If you answered questions one through eight in the affirmative, you are currently operating on a fixed mindset. If you answered questions nine through 16 in the affirmative, you have a growth mindset.

Don't panic if you are of the fixed mindset, you already picked up this book which means you are eager to problem-solve, and that's a key habit you will be developing as you make your way through these pages.

You may not believe it yet, but someone with a fixed mindset *can* change. The important thing is to recognize it is a mindset that can and must change if you are to become a successful entrepreneur.

Do you already have a growth mindset? Good for you, but as you already know, there is still room for improvement, growth and learning. In fact, if you are 100% growth mindset, you are eager and passionate about learning and excited about the information awaiting you in the next few chapters!

Why Does it Matter?

Perhaps you're not quite convinced that you need a growth mindset. Maybe you feel that it is better to just continue demonstrating your mastery of specific skills or traits? Perhaps you feel that "tried and true" methods or approaches should be all that is needed. Maybe you are of the belief that you shouldn't be challenged as you endeavor out into the world of entrepreneurialism, but simply asked to do your best in your specific area of expertise.

Let's look at this in an entirely different light. Let's look at it through the filter of "dieting". Yes, it seems like a peculiar comparison or analogy, but it is actually spot on...

A Simple Illustration

Most of us might begin dieting because we feel it would be better to weigh less. No matter what the reason (a special event, health, bathing suit season or general dissatisfaction with our weight), we will follow some tried and true methods.

We might limit calories, do exercise and wait for the pounds to melt away. We may see that progress is too slow, so we just do more of dieting and exercise to force weight loss, and while we do it, we may be thinking about how difficult it is to sustain this approach.

When we reach our goal after long weeks or months of hard work and dietary restraint, we relax our efforts. In fact, most of us often return (whether immediately or within a short period of time), to eating and behaving as we did before the weight loss.

The result? We fail in some way. We might regain weight, lose the strength and fitness we were able to achieve, or fail to see our new behaviors changed into permanent habits.

And here is where you might draw some clear lines between fixed and growth mindsets. How? Well, we did not only fail to keep the weight off, but we failed to *learn from the experience.* We might have been great at following the rules, adhering to the plan and doing the exercises needed, but we did not make new habits that ensured our optimal success.

The fixed mindset does this to us. It tells us that only a certain amount of change is possible (if any) and even effectively blocks us from learning and getting better at certain skills or traits.

If we stick to the dieting analogy, a fixed mindset doesn't let you challenge yourself and stick to it, even if there are some initial failures. The fixed mindset might say, "fine, I guess I'm meant to be at this weight!" and that's that.

It is a main reason that people who are dieting and have a "slip" (such as eating foods not included in the diet plan), but then continue to consume those foods in a binge or simply returning to their original way of eating. If they couldn't do it successfully and without failure, well, forget it, they just can't.

Realize that you must, instead, develop (note, that says *develop* and not *already have*) a mindset that embraces the challenges and sees them as opportunities for learning and growth.

The dieter with the growth mindset would see that the pounds are coming off slowly, and wonder if there were functional tweaks that could help. They would talk to a fitness person to find out if more weight resistance would be better for long term success or a nutritionist to find out if there are flaws in their food choices. They would consider using modern tech to support goals and make new habits (food journaling, eating a specific hours, and even enjoying cheats to ensure success).

Learning and growing rather than seeking to flawlessly execute whatever known skills.. .that is the difference at work here, and in fixed versus growth mindsets.

In essence, shifting from the "all or nothing" of the fixed mindset, to the "what is to be gained from this" of the growth mindset is one of the dominating characteristics of all successful entrepreneurs.

It is only when you have the growth mindset that you can start to define, develop and stick to the habits that will make you a successful entrepreneur. In fact, when your mindset changes, these habits become second nature and you may not find yourself in need of reminders to take certain steps, respond certain ways and more.

Changing a Mindset

So, you come up as having a fixed mindset? Maybe you answered only some of the questions like someone with a fixed mindset and want to be sure you are developing or strengthening the more successful growth mindset.

Either way, it all starts with recognizing *how your mindset is currently affecting you*, or more accurately, how it *affects your thoughts and thought processes*.

Remember, your mindset is what frames your interpretation of all that is happening around you.

At any given moment, our minds are tracking everything that's happening, interpreting it, and calculating what to do. Your mindset is not something that turns on and off only when contemplating your business pursuits or other actions - your mindset is a 24/7 filter of everything in life - from work and relationships to what you eat and what you believe.

As a simple illustration, here is mindset at work: You are sitting on the sofa watching TV. You hear the teapot whistle, and you know you will need to get up to shut it off, make tea and come back to relax. You might feel a surge of fatigue because you recalled the day and this leads you to thinking, with resentment, about the issues that caused this sense of tiredness - traffic, kids, colleagues, work, and so on. You are also going to be thinking of things perhaps cued by what is on the TV, just outside the window and in your thoughts (such as an argument with a friend or discussion with a colleague).

You will always be thinking several things at once, and all of it is going to be colored or interpreted through the fixed or growth mindset.

Your mind will always be interpreting, monitoring and cycling through everything at a fast pace, but there are times when your perspective is a bit skewed or flawed. When it is, you might have some faulty interpretations of things that are happening or have already occurred. You might experience strong emotional responses such as anger, sadness or even a sense of smugness.

For instance, as you make your way to the kitchen to turn off the kettle, you trip over someone's shoes, you get angry at the owner of the shoes. You think about something a colleague said, and you think a negative thought about them, like "how dare he critique my work on that assignment!" You look at the color of the kitchen walls and think of how you do/don't like that color.

Lots of emotions and lots of judgments are going on, and it *happens all of the time*. And it is your mindset that is going to be doing most of this, serving as a framework into which your interpretations are poured.

It could be why you re-hash an embarrassing situation from days earlier or why you are absolutely certain that people are judging you and feeling superior to you. This, however, is the fixed mindset, and it is dominated by thoughts oriented towards judgment - judging others as well as yourself.

Fortunately, this can be remedied.

How? The good news is that it is not rocket science, reinventing the wheel or climbing Mt. Everest to begin changing your fixed mindset to a growth one. Before we look at steps to use in order to begin the shift from fixed to growth - let's consider how a growth mindset interprets things.

It, too, is a mindset dominated by monitoring, but what the growth mindset does is take the information and considers how to learn from it or take positive actions based on the data. For example, the person with the growth mindset will encounter information and think something along the lines of "what should I learn from this?" or "what can be improved to avoid this outcome in the future?" It is all about constructive interpretation.

So, instead of becoming annoyed by someone leaving their shoes in the way, the person with a growth mindset will think of how they can deal with that person to encourage better habits. When considering the color of the kitchen, the growth mindset will ponder ways of enhancing a color they like or downplaying a hue they dislike, if repainting is not an option. They may even view the issue as not worthy of the time it would take to consider it…"the kitchen is blue, but I don't want to waste energy worrying about it today".

It is a problem solving mindset dominated by energizing and positive "inner monologues". There will never be thoughts like "I'm a total failure at this" or "he/she is a complete failure" or "just who do they think they are criticizing me?"

And it is first hearing, then recognizing and taming that inner voice that is the first step towards changing the fixed mindset permanently. Let's look at the key tactics you need to use in order to so.

Inner Monologues

How do you feel if you experience a setback of some sort?

You didn't get the job, you ate a few too many sweets over the weekend and you're dieting, or you received less than glowing comments on a project. these are all ways of experiencing a setback, and how you think about them typically also involves some sort of inner monologue.

It could be an "inner voice", the way you do "self speak" or countless other ways of describing the actual thoughts that you "hear" when you experience a setback.

The person with a fixed mindset never hears anything but negative ideas: "You failed this time, so you are a failure" or "If you don't put yourself out there you won't be at risk for rejection or a loss of self-esteem" or "Don't be a fraud.you don't have that talent/skill/etc".

Your inner monologue does not just speak out once about a setback and it also never forgets. So, you might also hear yourself thinking things like "If you were meant to do that." or "If you were talented enough for that." or even "Just quit and save your dignity." over and over.

You should also realize that it is the fixed mindset that likes to point a finger of blame for setbacks. We already saw this when we explained how a fixed mindset thinks things like, "Who do they think they are criticizing me?" or "It's not my fault it failed, it was X, Y or Z's fault." Passing the blame verifies your belief, your negative belief. It allows you to remain fixed in hearing criticisms or seeing failure when you could be growing and learning.

However, most of these inner monologues can be re-tuned to the far more productive growth mindset. For instance, that "criticism" just mentioned is probably more along the lines of feedback or suggestions, and even if phrased badly or with an unpleasant manner, can often be seen for what it truly is - insight.

Think about it for a moment. Let's say you are hearing feedback (whether it is constructive or very matter of fact). You have two ways of "hearing" it.

- *The first is the fixed mindset's way, which involves feeling some sort of emotional response, usually upset, anger or shame.*

- *The other way is hearing it as constructive information. Rather than getting angry, the growth mindset mentally "leans in" to get the most out of what is being said.*

So, the first tactic to use in order to turnaround your mindset is to listen to what your inner monologue says, and recognize when it is revealing a fixed mindset. If you cannot hear, see or experience something without a judgmental inner voice standing up to be heard, you need to tame it.

The good news is that taming it is as easy as choosing to do so, and that is what brings us to the second tactic...

Choosing Growth

Life, as we hear quite often, is all about choices. What jobs we do, how we eat or live, what activities or hobbies.life does involve many options. However, the choice we need to focus on here revolves around your interpretation of events, challenges, criticisms, setbacks and more.

In other words: *How do you choose to react to anything?*

It is said that we have control over nothing, *except* how we react to things. So, we have no control over a person being difficult, but we do have a choice in how we respond. We also have no control over setbacks or challenges, but we most certainly do have choices in how we respond, perceive and react.

If you found out that you have a fixed mindset, or you are simply working on building the strongest mindset for success, then you must learn to choose the best way to react or respond.

As a very basic illustration of this, consider hearing some criticism of a proposal or a project you have been working on. You can choose two very different ways to see, hear and respond to the criticism:

1. You can interpret the comments as validation of your belief that you weren't cut out to do that job. You will blame it on the fact that you don't have the ability or talent to do it or on someone else involved. You can hear yourself being called a failure. In other words, that criticism or commentary had to be nothing but praise or you felt a failure - it is the all or nothing at work, and that is the fixed mindset.

2. You can interpret the comments as proof that you need to regroup and try harder or use a different approach. You accept that you may need to hone your skills, extend yourself a bit to make that extra effort, and put even more energy into the effort or strategy. You don't even think of words like "failure", but instead look at how you can really own your work and see it through to a better outcome. It is the gaining-through-any-learning-experience approach at work here, and that is the growth mindset.

"Okay," you think, "I can see the dramatic differences, but *how* do I get from number one to number two? How do I start changing how I react or respond?"

We already took steps to have you recognize when your inner voice was using that defeatist fixed mindset. So, that's the first way to begin changing.

Once you *hear* these things, you can then *apply your free will* (the ability to choose), to react differently.

It would be as simple as this: You are writing your first blog and send it out to a few friends to read before you post it to your social media and other sites. One of them has a few things to say about your grammar and the structure of the blog, and you don't like what you hear. Your immediate reaction may be "He doesn't know what he's talking about? Let him try to write a blog! I spent hours on it and he's just written off half my work with a few nasty comments!"

Now, in the middle of all of this noise, you can choose to stop thinking like this, and redirect your thoughts towards growth. Instead, you might think, "Okay, I asked him to comment and he's saying that I wasn't very clear in this part of the blog and that I should rearrange paragraphs to make it easier to read. I'll try that and re-test it with a few other people to see what they say."

You *choose to learn and grow* rather than allowing judgmental and emotional responses steer you away from success and growth.

That means you are now:

- *Listening for the unhelpful mindset*
- *Choosing to respond differently*
- *Perhaps already thinking of some ready-made reactions to help you get past such moments*

In fact, this is the third tactic...

Positive Self-Talk

A 2016 report in Psychology Today said that you can "overwrite the negative voice with positive truths." Naturally, that means you need to know those truths in order to continually overwrite the unwanted messages.

As the report explained, though, "Positive self-talk is not self-deception. It is not mentally looking at circumstances with eyes that see only what you want to see. Rather, positive self-talk is about recognizing the truth, in situations and in yourself. One of the fundamental truths is that you will make mistakes. To expect perfection in yourself or anyone else is unrealistic. To expect no difficulties in life, whether through your own actions or sheer circumstances, is also unrealistic."

So, take some time now to composed messages that counteract whatever negative reactions and responses your fixed mindset kicks out at you each day or whenever you face challenges. These truths are always there, because all negative messages automatically have an equal and opposite message.

Here are a few examples:

- *"Can't you do anything right?" versus "Each time I learn from a mistake or failure, I get closer to success"*

- *"You don't really have the natural talent for this..." versus "I am a beginner right now, and I know with time and effort I can learn how to do this."*

- *"If you fail, everyone is going to think of you as a total failure" versus "Name one successful person.guess what.they had plenty of failures, too"*

- *"If you don't try, you don't open yourself up to failure, shame or embarrassment" versus "If you don't try, you are automatically failing"*

- *"All of this would be so easy if you were meant to be doing it and if you had the skills or talents for it" versus "Nothing comes easy, and it takes commitment, effort , passion and practice to get good at anything"*

- *"This failure is not my fault, it is due to someone or something else" versus "If I don't admit my part in this failure, I won't be able to improve the situation and I won't learn anything from all of my effort."*

Don't worry if your truths are just a few words (i.e. "onward and upward"), it is more about having something to say back to that inner voice that can lead you back towards success.

Whenever you suffer a setback, experience a challenge or hear criticism or feedback, know that your fixed mindset is probably going to speak up. Be ready and choose to react with your growth-oriented truths.

Even just reviewing the things your inner monologue seems to repeatedly throw out at you is a great way to begin making growth mindset choices instead. You are going to become more and more aware of the power of the fixed mindset and then overcome it and really start to manifest success. And that takes us to the final tactic...

The Mindset in Action

Look at anyone who has succeeded and you are likely looking at someone who has the growth mindset, and their success is evidence of that mindset in action. These are people who (consciously or not) have opted to listen to the more productive mindset and who may have even made choosing to speak truths to themselves their regular habit.

To begin developing the mindset and habits of successful entrepreneurs means choosing to use a growth mindset at all times. That means you need to choose to listen to that inner voice, and have answers to counteract any negative comments that voice makes. In time, you will re-train it to say what you wish it to say.

Until then, you can just remember that three of the most crucial qualities of successful entrepreneurs are also greatly harmed by the fixed mindset. So, whenever you encounter the following issues, be particularly in tune with your inner voice and be ready with your truths if you wish to keep moving towards success:

- *When you are facing a challenge and you feel an unwillingness to take it on unreservedly.*

- *When you suffer a setback and refrain from trying again due to all of the negative comments rattling around your thoughts.*

- *When you hear any sort of feedback or criticism and you opt to defend yourself or your dignity first, instead of listening to or acting on the suggestions, guidance or advice offered.*

It can so often feel like your mind is in control and entirely separate from your will, goals or wishes. That, however, is not the case. It comes down to developing your mindset like you would any habit - keep repeating and practicing it until it becomes second nature and something you do without conscious thought or even effort.

The result of this shift in mindset is crucial, as journalist Tom McKay wrote, "In the long run, fixed minds will achieve less. ..Challenges help [those with growth mindset] improve and setbacks ultimately motivate [them] to work harder and move forward."

And moving forward is the one sure-fire way to achieve success, no matter what entrepreneurial pursuit you have in mind!

Now that you understand the mindset of all successful entrepreneurs (and successful people in general, for that matter), let's turn our attention and energies towards developing similar *habits*.

Chapter Two

Habits

"Successful people are simply those with successful habits."

- Brian Tracy

The Habits of the Successful Entrepreneur

It would be very simple to look at the world's most successful entrepreneurs, and even those unknown in the wider world but still successful in their own businesses, and see some common traits or behaviors. For example, a shortlist of qualities of successful entrepreneurs would have to include:

- *Passion*
- *Adaptability*
- *Self-discipline*
- *Persistence*
- *Competence*
- *Determination*
- *Resilience*
- *Confidence*
- *Fearlessness*

Eagerness to learn

Refusing to quit

- *Excellence in communication*

- *Skilled in sales or promotion*

These are "traits", though, and not necessarily "habits".

Habits, as defined by Merriam-Webster can be a "manner of conducting oneself" or a "prevailing disposition or character of a person's thoughts and feelings".

For our purposes, we are considering different habits. We need to look at habits that are "a settled tendency or usual manner of behavior ... a behavior pattern acquired by frequent repetition or physiologic exposure that shows itself in regularity or increased facility of performance .an acquired mode of behavior that has become nearly or completely involuntary."

And it is without a doubt that some of the world's most successful do have modes of behavior that are nearly involuntary and the result of repetition. Habits, for most successful people are not automatic or natural but cultivated for very specific reasons.

As one article in Entrepreneur said of habits of the most successful entrepreneurs, "For you to find success, find something that best suits you and turn it into a habit." That is actually a very wise recommendation.

How do you do it? Let's figure that out.

You and Your Entrepreneurial Habits

Quick.visualize yourself as a success at whatever enterprise you have in mind.

Now, imagine a typical day in which you are working and growing your business. To make the most of this exercise, really visualize as much as you can. For example

What time do you plan on getting up?

What would your morning involve?

How are you actually working? Is it at home, an office or varied locations?

Are you going to focus on one specific area of your business and assign out duties to others, or handle everything with a bit of oversight into each aspect of the company?

What type of boss are you going to be?

What about down time...what are your plans for time spent not working?

Did you envision being free of work and letting a company run itself?

As you can see, your vision for your future is going to be very different from the plans or goals others have for themselves. The reason for this exercise is to show you that you already have some habits in mind (such as waking at 8AM and doing a workout before going to the office, and so on).

Unfortunately, your intended habits may not be in line with those of the most successful entrepreneurs. It is incredibly useful to understand some of the key habits that occur in the day to day lives of the successful. Why? Because they are not as "general" as you might think.

For example, Facebook co-founder and youthful wonder kid Mark Zuckerberg says that he makes a habit of minimizing low-impact decisions - how? He eliminates a decision all of us are forced to make every day - what to wear. Instead of sweating this particular, almost zero-impact decision, he actually wears the same "uniform" every day. He opts for jeans, plain t-shirts and a hoodie. Steve Jobs did something similar, wearing jeans and a black turtleneck to the office daily.

Do people like Oprah or Richard Branson also choose uniform-like outfits as part of their effective daily habits? No. This doesn't suit their goals or objectives. They probably do look for ways to optimize their time, but a habit of wearing the same types of garments over and over is not one way they achieve that aim.

The point is that the habits you develop have to serve you best.

In the previous chapter we made a pointed effort of identifying your type of mindset and then developing some "truths" to use against any negative, fixed mindset chatter. As an example, you might think "I don't have the level of knowledge to make this a success". Your growth mindset response is to recognize the thought for what it is and then counteract it with something like, "Well, I don't have it now, but can obtain it by doggedly pursuing information, guidance and learning. I can then use it towards success."

Guess what? You can also make this a habit! Reading, studying, speaking with others about the subject...these are things to turn into daily habits that get you to your goal and ensure you succeed as an entrepreneur of any kind. In fact, we just mentioned Oprah Winfrey - and learning something each day is one of her empowering habits.

You too can choose to make it habitual to sketch out an hour a day to read about your industry or spend an hour a day taking an online course. You can book one consultation a week with an expert or mentor and learn even more. These steps can become regular parts of your routine (i.e. habits), allowing you to continually build on your knowledge through ongoing reading, consults and learning.

Because it can still be tough to figure out which types of habits to develop, we are going to do a review of more than ten of the habits that the world's most successful entrepreneurs have claimed. You can then pick and choose according to your needs, goals, feelings and priorities. The point is to develop your growth mindset with habits that are most ideally suited to your success.

Habits to Develop

"Continuous learning is the minimum requirement for success in any field."

-Dennis Waitley

Before we begin looking at important habits of successful entrepreneurs, let's once again look at the definition of the word. Recall that the definitions we used included words like "acquired", "repetition" and "involuntary". This means you cannot just choose certain habits and they magically manifest in your behaviors. Rather, it becomes a case of practice makes perfect.

It is also important to remember that not all of the habits will, necessarily, apply to you. Certainly don't convince yourself to hold off on pursuing your goals as a business entrepreneur until you are automatically using the habits you select, either. Try to be fluid in how you practice and apply them, and always be ready to change course if it will help.

As that quote above reminds us, your habits should be a constant source of learning. Learning what works and what doesn't, learning what aspect of any habit supports or does not support goals, and constantly gauging how much, or little, certain habits are helping you move forward are ways you will learn.

Early to Bed, Early to Rise...

Benjamin Franklin is easily one of the most famous success stories in history. Not only a founder of the United States, but a remarkably effective inventor, scientist, farmer and diplomat.

He is famous, too, for his many quotes (most from *Poor Richard's Almanack* published in 1709) including the one above. In its entirety, it reads "Early to bed and early to rise, makes a man healthy, wealthy and wise".

In addition to sticking with a strict sleeping schedule, Franklin was noted for his adherence to a very rigid daily routine. As one source notes, he "followed a 13-week self-improvement plan where he focused on one virtue (habit) per week" and he continually cycled through this routine four times each year. It included times when he would wake and go to bed as well as his activities in each two to four hour window of time.

Others who do the same include Tesla Motors founder Elon Musk who is noted for his daily schedule that is broken out into five minute intervals. This enables him to get the very most from any hour or day. He also schedules specific work for specific days. For example, he may only focus on Tesla two days per week and his other ventures on separate days.

We also already mentioned Zuckerberg who eliminates time spent making no- productive decisions by committing to a basic wardrobe that allows him to dress in moments and without thought.

In both Zuckerberg's and Musk's examples, they indicate that they stick to a rigid routine and schedule for one ultimate goal - to get the most out of their work day, emphasizing important ideas or thoughts and eliminating wasted time on non-productive or nonessential issues.

This shows a blend of habits designed to support productivity, efficiency, and more. You might also consider **habits that minimize many typical, daily choices**. Some options include eating the same lunch or breakfast each day, choosing a specific goal for each day of the week (much like fitness enthusiasts do, i.e. "leg day", and so on), and **living by "if-then" rules.**

This last one is a great habit because it gives you flexibility and works like this: "You're much more likely to follow through on your good intentions if you use if-then planning: if X happens, then I will do Y. The if-then allows you to decide your course of action in advance, before you're tired, stressed, or swamped."

In fact, this is such an empowering habit, you may want to make it entirely independent of this point and consider it as one of the top recommendations on its own.

Before moving on, let's also consider Franklin's advice about early rising again. Some experts have indicated that "the way people handle the first 10 minutes of the workday can largely determine how productive and effective they'll be the rest of the day." The report went on to emphasize that early rising tied into this, saying "the daily habits of successful business leaders such as T-Mobile's John Legere to Chobani's Hamdi Ulukaya. ..found that not one of them woke up later than 7 a.m."

Getting up early and **sticking to a fixed schedule built on productivity** are two excellent habits to consider developing if you are eager to nurture your success.

Knowledge is Power.and Insight and Guidance, Too!

Another report on the habits of successful entrepreneurs pointed out that many put "reading books at the top of their to-do lists". Keep in mind, people with the growing mindset are passionate about learning, and especially when a topic relates to their area of interest.

Billionaire Warren Buffett is living proof of the value of reading a lot about your field. He says he currently spends around 80% of his days reading, and none of it is for entertainment. Like all successful entrepreneurs, he reads to learn.

However, before you say "sure, he can read most of the day...he's a billionaire", keep in mind that he read up to one thousand pages each day when he was just beginning his career in investing and finance.

As you might guess, Oprah Winfrey (with her enormously famous book club) has been a passionate devotee of reading for most of her life. She says that "books were my pass to personal freedom" and took her reading habit and turned it into an enormously profitable part of her empire.

World-class philanthropist and Microsoft CEO Bill Gates says that he tries to read a book each week and credits reading with inspiring, informing and driving many of his endeavors.

So, seek ways to **enhance your knowledge generally and specifically** as one of your new habits.

Of course, knowledge doesn't only come from consuming lots of books and reading materials. Making it a habit to **remain open to new ideas** of others around you is another way to gain knowledge.

You can also find out about the thoughts of others by seeking guidance. Guidance, in fact, is so important to success, that we are going to look at it as a separate habit altogether.

Seeking Guidance

Finding and working with a mentor is not really a habit so much as it is a step or tactic, so we don't want to delve into the concept of mentoring here. What we do want to emphasize, though, is the importance of **seeking guidance as a habit**.

Remember, at the beginning of this chapter we said that you might realize you need more knowledge, skill or other information to become a successful entrepreneur. That might mean that you should train yourself to regularly seek guidance as a "knee jerk reaction".

Why? One of the most harmful habits a professional might make is isolating themselves or trying to handle everything on their own. While it is a recipe for disaster, it also effectively prevents you from ever learning anything. When you make it a habit to consistently seek guidance, you nip this issue permanently in the bud.

And just where should you seek guidance? The answer is also a habit, because you must also **develop the habit of cultivating an array of "sources".**

As one expert explained, "Countless successful entrepreneurs will tell you they could not have accomplished their goals without help from their own personal guru." So, a professor, colleague, former boss, friend or expert in the field willing to give you time may be an ideal choice. Retired entrepreneurs are amazing channels for guidance and advice, and you may want to find out if you have any way of accessing such a unique resource for guidance.

In fact, SCORE exists with just this in mind. It was once known as the Service Corps of Retired Executives but has since been updated to mean the Counselors to America's Small Business and offers free mentoring. With local chapters as well as online options, it is a fantastic way to get accurate, valuable and useful guidance.

However, there are also print resources you need to consider. For example, use sites like Amazon or your library's website to look for reading lists relating to the top books in your subject or industry.

For instance, if you are thinking about a business relating to low-cost app design, read as much as you can about the industry and any biographies or non-fiction books relating to that field.

Keep in mind, though, that this habit is not just about always asking for advice or building on your base of knowledge or skill. Just like those entrepreneurs who make a point of reading all of the time, the **key to making the most of seeking guidance "is absorbing the knowledge, translating it and putting it into practice." Make this a habit, too.**

Think of seeking advice less as troubleshooting and more as growing your abilities to become the same sort of resource you turn to now.

Become Connected

In addition to making it a habit of seeking guidance or advice, you also need to **make a habit of seeking connection** with others in your field, or even those operating in related but not directly connected fields.

Recognizing the value of connection is itself a habit as you may meet someone you don't even think of as involved in your industry, yet that same person could prove a valuable link in your chain towards success. In fact, you will find this is true of many different people. We already determined the need to make a habit of being open to what others say, and this spills over into connecting with others, too.

Are we talking strictly about networking? No, we are speaking about networking in addition to other areas of connection. Your audience, as a prime example, must feel connected to you through your business or enterprise. It is exactly why social media pages for most businesses are now a must - but only if you are actively engaging with your audience, creating connection, through them.

Your employees (if you have them) must feel free to speak to you about ideas or changes - and you must **make a habit of listening** and considering what they say.

Let's look at the other specific habits you should consider developing where connectivity is concerned.

Networking is the likeliest place to begin, and it involves a lot of dedication and even a touch of ambition.

After all, you are going to pursue a connection or link to people who are probably major players in your industry. However, as one expert explains, "As an entrepreneur, networking should be a high priority that is enjoyable, but also thought of as crucial to personal growth and business development."

It is never just about being able to say you are "linked" to famous movers and shakers. It is about actually creating those links, creating that "network" which gives its name to the activity in the first place. **Habitually interacting with like-minded people** and those working in your field will enlighten you as well as connect you.

Consider that any groups or organizations you join can provide you with vital word of mouth, but it can also align you with people who can offer all kinds of advice or guidance, and even support. They might be able to refer your business or help open doors to key players, suppliers or thinkers in your field.

Where should you begin networking? The Internet has websites like LinkedIn, but also more creative options like Meetup.com which can put you in touch with people who might be doing activities or meeting to discuss a lot of relevant issues.

Don't forget to join the Chamber of Commerce as this is a top notch way to network. Look into your industry, follow or friend those in the spotlight, and read what they have to say. **Respond**, too, because even billionaire entrepreneurs like Richard Branson still look at this sort of information. He might even answer your question!

Another way to connect is to remember the very reason you are an entrepreneur - there was a need that you recognized and then created a solution to fill it with. Because of that, you have to **constantly network with your customers**. It is one of the few ways you have to demonstrate that they are a priority and not just a paycheck.

If you don't quite buy into this idea, consider Twitter. Founders Jack Dorsey, Evan Williams and Biz Stone dedicated a lot more time during the startup phase to optimizing usability than worrying about earnings. The result is one of the easiest to use networks with enormous revenues and success.

As one article explains, "they built a world-changing communication engine in which his users feel like they have ownership." And they did this by communicating and networking directly with them.

Lastly, you can build connections by **habitually meeting new people**. You can do this in the real world or online, but the point is you are always looking for those who can teach you new things or help you with your entrepreneurial pursuit. This habit is not as simple as it sounds because it means you will have to actively go out of our way to identify and find new people to meet. You could do this at Chamber meetings, participating in conferences or seminars, arranging your own seminars, through related groups and more.

They Face Fear

Whether you are strongly risk-averse or you believe yourself to be relatively unafraid of risk, the simplest truth is that fearlessness needs to become a habit. Whether it is facing the fear of risking your savings, finding yourself the main decision maker, or just fear of failure, you have to **make it a habit to look fear in the eye and keep right on walking past it.**

Of course, there is another facet to this, and it is to **make it a habit to assess your decisions when fear is part of the issue**. Why? Because fear is so potent that it can really drive our decisions and lead us far off the mark. Here's an interesting quote from an article in Medium: "Too many would-be entrepreneurs operate with a scarcity mindset rather than approaching business from a place of abundance."

What does that mean? Instead of saying, "I wish I could attend that seminar, but I just can't afford that trip" try reworking the response. For instance, "what can I do, starting today, to earn the cash I need for the seminar?"

Yes, it is a **habit of always reframing your thoughts**, which is (as you might recall) a way of shifting your mindset!

As another example, consider this negative money-oriented thought: "I have to handle everything in this startup because I don't have the funds to hire help". Reframing it into a positive solution like, "Well, my hourly rate potential really offsets anything I'd pay a virtual assistant..." shows a workable, reasonable and non-fear based decision.

Accept...EXPECT to Fail

Rather than just tell you to make "bracing for failure" a habit, let's consider it in much more positive ways.

First and foremost, **make it a habit to see failures** always, and perhaps it should be read ALWAYS, **as learning experiences**. This is the most common sense approach to anything, life, entrepreneurial activities, romance.everything.

Just think about this, "Babe Ruth struck out at the plate 1330 times. He didn't let that stop him because in recorded history he continues to be in the top five for the most home runs of all time with 714."

Clearly, the man was learning with each time at bat, even if it was a defeat. One great way to look at small to large failures is this - it is never fatal because it always opens the door to a different path or opportunity. Make a habit of learning from failure, and you actually never fail.

Let's also look at being prepared to fail as **habitually being ready and willing to shift gears**. Why not just stick to the idea that failure happens? Because that sounds too much like the end of the story - it failed, oh well, next idea! This is *not* what we suggest you make a habit of thinking or doing.

Instead, when your efforts don't pay off in the ways you expected and/or hoped, it is a successful entrepreneur that simply tries something different. As an article in Entrepreneur said, "Many incredible businesses and services are the second, third or even fourth attempt of an entrepreneur who just flat out refused to give up and instead decided to try something different."

Remember, a major part of your work as an entrepreneur is to "define, invest, build, repeat", but as you are defining and building, you will make a habit of assessing and evaluating many different components of that business or idea, and respond constructively.

When something seems to be amiss - maybe you defined the audience incorrectly, maybe you choose the wrong goal, it could be any number of issues - the successful entrepreneurs come at the issue from a new and different angle. Make a **habit out of being willing to admit you were wrong and adjust course**.

Of course, this habit of anticipating hurtles and failures also means you have a need to adapt. Make **adapting to any number of different demands or scenarios a major habit**. This looks back at the "if-then" habit we mentioned earlier, but also throws in a need to be emotionally flexible, too.

As an example, in the midst of a product launch, some sort of marketing curveball comes at you. What do you do? The habit of being adaptable means you will have prepared some different steps or responses - even if it is simply "don't panic" and/or "okay, think this through". This will allow you to make good decisions even in the thick of things - including a failure or major setback.

Of course, if you make a habit of preparing for accepting that failure is a reality, you also have to **make a habit of holding yourself accountable**. The very best leaders are those who take the ultimate responsibility for anything that occurs - even if a direct link cannot be connected to them. Why is that? The entrepreneur picks everyone on the team, and if one link in that chain is flawed, it must be the result of the leader's decision making process.

This is also why you must **make a habit of surrounding yourself with a fantastic team**. The team must include mentors or people who can provide guidance, there should be some serious accountability partners who hold you to your word, and you must make it a habit to choose only those who can help the enterprise - never your ego. If you surround yourself with the proverbial "yes" people, you will fail.

Be a Planner

Of course, if you adhere to the "if-then" habit, you will also already be making a **habit of planning ahead.** While we indicated that you should be flexible and adaptable, that does not mean you should wander without some sort of road map or general plan for success.

Remember that Elon Musk maps out each day in five minute intervals and chooses a goal oriented theme for each day. You can create a similar approach by planning your days, but successful entrepreneurs go well beyond that. One thing they share in common where planning is concerned is in short and long term goals. **Make a habit of simply becoming a goal oriented person.**

Identify and write down goals, put them into a logical order, and then make a habit of focusing on goals and align your effort and attentions in order to achieve them. This is where some of that flexibility may be put to use because you are going to have to continually evaluate where your work is taking you.

Think of the website Classtivity. ..its founder Payal Kadakia continually evaluated goals and realized that her initial plans had put the firm on track towards the wrong goal. She willingly switched gears and took all the information obtained to create new and far more effective goals. This resulted in the creation of the ClassPass website and it was due almost entirely to the **founder's habit of creating short term, midterm and long term goals, assessing them and shifting course if needed**.

Remember, though, it can be very challenging to control yourself if things don't seem to be going as you had hoped or planned. This is why you must make a **habit of acting purposefully and being patient** about the outcomes. Nothing is instantaneous, and your fear of failure could drive you to make flawed choices or plans. If you calmly map out your route with short, mid and long term goals, if-then plans, and times for review and adjustment, you can keep your progress steady.

Also, make a **habit of checking your focus**. What does that mean? It means being very clear on goals at all times. While those moments of panic just described above can be to blame for your loss of focus, so too can distractions like new projects or tasks others can handle. Habitually be sure you are not overly focused on details that pull your energies away from the actual goals.

A simple example of this is the entrepreneur who gets overly focused on the design of a newsletter, dedicating too many hours to reconsidering column sizes, colors, graphics and other details. These are distractions that cut into the time and energy you could be devoting elsewhere, and which most certainly take you off track of the goals you must meet to be a success.

Don't forget to **form the habit of "time off", too**. It is a simple truth that if you don't plan for any time off, you are planning to crash, burn and fail. Without some time to regroup, clear the mind and re-energize, you are making it almost a certainty that you will make major mistakes.

One expert has this to say, "Successful entrepreneurs understand that breaks are necessary and can help facilitate innovation and hard work when it's really necessary."

As odd as it may seem to you now, it is important to make down time a habit just as much as work time.

Be Innovative

One of the key traits of a successful entrepreneur is that they are always confident. This allows them to get the work done - even when they feel stressed or strained.

Confidence is what allows someone to see the opportunity when others see nothing but risk or challenge. Yet, that, as noted is a trait.

How do you convert confidence from a trait to a habit? You do it through vision and innovation. It takes a great deal of confidence to build something around your own personal vision, and it takes even more confidence to innovate. Why? Because you are breaking the established models in certain ways if your entrepreneurial pursuit is unique or innovative. Yet, all successful entrepreneurs have done just that, so you too must make it a **habit to develop your own vision and innovate around it.**

What this, fundamentally means is that you have to trust yourself 100%. That can be scary for many people, but if you foster that growth mindset within yourself, you can see past fear, lack of self-confidence and past failures. Begin simply by strengthening your trust in yourself, which is a bit easier than it sounds.

How? You have this entrepreneurial idea, right? What do you see your customers needing? No matter what the answer, realize that your instinct has let you see their needs even before they have appeared.

Now, it is your job to manifest that solution to their needs. You are the right one for this job, even of many others have already tried and failed. This is because you have made a **habit of sharpening your vision through other habits** (assessment, flexibility, listening, and so on).

Of course, innovation is also about creative solutions. This too is an enormous part of success, but it is often something that has to be worked into a habit. Most of us already know a lot of tried and true solutions to different issues. However, it is the entrepreneur who makes a **habit of seeking creative solutions** who usually goes the farthest. In the end, it won't just be creative problem solving that you gain from such a habit, it will also be innovation and vision, too.

Not in It for the Money. At Least, Not Only for the Money

What is one of the most well-known bits of advice given to baseball players? It is "keep your eye on the ball". It makes sense, and yet it is also a habit of very effective entrepreneurs, too.

What we mean is simple: The successful entrepreneurs would usually agree that they are not in it entirely for the money. Most say that they are in it for the last part of that four-word formula we have used several times: Define, invest, build, repeat. The "repeat" or even the "exit" is something that many entrepreneurs focus on.

How does this lead to success? When you **make a habit of keeping your eye on the exit**, you will often be able to navigate more clearly to that point. Whether exit means selling or handing over control to others, or even going public, you may find that focusing there helps you succeed more than focusing on the bottom line.

Certainly, no one gets into any sort of business without considering profitability. Yet, if all you can focus on is the earnings, it can lead you down the wrong path. As the simplest example, consider that you are looking to monetize your blog. You look only at the most immediate ways to grow the audience. This might mean you expand social media, PPC ads and email marketing.

However, someone else, who makes a habit of looking towards the exit, might see that a more obvious stepping stone is a vlog or a podcast, or even an app associated with the product or company.

Science actually backs this up through a study done on the impact of monetary focus on the human psyche. What it had to say is surprising, "it can be concluded that financial gain is not the primary driver of great entrepreneurs..."

Instead, the data explains, it is "extra-rational motivations", those psychological rather than tangible, that drive entrepreneurs. What are those motivations? Competition and its thrills, a yearning for adventure, the joys of creating something, the satisfaction of building a team, and even a desire to feel more meaning in life are but some of those motivations.

So, if you want to emulate successful entrepreneurs, set aside an emphasis on earnings, and simply make a **habit of focusing on the exit, success or even process of building your business**.

Yes, running any business is certainly about making money and profits, but if you focus too intensely on that, it can blur your perspective. Simply making a habit of keeping your aim or focus on something beyond and/or past the money is a much clearer path to success.

Embrace Being a Rookie

Many successful entrepreneurs have been able to succeed because they really owned their novice or "rookie" status as they began. This is a way to develop a unique company culture (remember that Twitter example earlier, in which we considered their focus on functionality rather than profits) and it can easily become a key to success.

Naturally, embracing your rookie-ness is not something you will do easily or with comfort. Why not? It is essentially saying that you will make a point of wearing your status as a point of pride, when most of us would rather look super professional. Yet, in doing that, you can come across as even more of an amateur than you are as well as missing out on some interesting opportunities.

A great example of this is the online clothing company known as ModCloth. Entirely unique and original, it's founder Susan Gregg Koger began the operating the firm before she was even 18 years old. She opened her shop without any retail experience, and rather than trying to copy others, she made a **habit of embracing her inexperience** and developing her plans around her own model, concept and intention. She wanted a social experience for her shoppers and she used creative problem solving and unusual outside of the box approaches to create an enormously successful site. And rather than steer away from this model, the company still relies heavily on this initial "culture" of rookie, novice, beginner or uninformed approaches to new and changing needs.

In short, make a **habit of making your own footprints rather than following those of others who came before you**. This is the essence of entrepreneurship and a clear trait in most major successes.

Another way to embrace being a beginner is to delegate whenever possible. Ask any successful entrepreneur and they automatically agree that you cannot do everything and succeed. Early on, most **make a habit to delegate** tasks they are not capable of doing well.

Obviously, your budget may prevent you from delegating much of anything, but just consider items like logos, landing pages, websites, some blog or social media content, or other similar tasks that are far better if a professional touch is applied.

You can embrace being a startup or newbie by simply focusing on what's most important, accepting that there are limits to what you can handle, and prioritizing. These things can be accomplished if you **make a habit of saying to yourself "I am not an**

expert yet, but can learn from the work of others" and you can only obtain these lessons by delegating whenever and wherever possible.

Know Thyself

At the beginning of this chapter we noted that you must look at the habits listed here and choose from those that best suit your goals or needs. By now, you might still be asking how anyone is supposed to figure out which of the habits are the most critical, vital or assuredly going to bring success. As one journalist wrote about habits and successful people, "which daily habits are critical to success, and which are personal preference and idiosyncrasy?"

One of the strongest habits of the successful, and one that can definitely help you choose the *other* important habits, is simply **making a habit of spending time to really know yourself.**

The most successful people have a much higher level of self-awareness than those who do not reach their goals.

For example, they know about personal energy and the importance of exercise, good diet and adequate rest. However, their knowledge of that goes beyond "get eight hours, eat your fruits and vegetables, and so on..."

They know exactly what exercise gets them going (for example, Mark Cuban does one hour of cardio almost every day of the week), what foods make them feel energized, and even what sort of environment is needed to trigger their productivity.

Successful people prioritize, and here too it is not just "what's the first thing I need to do today?" Instead, they choose priorities based on their mission, vision or purpose. And they asked themselves about priorities every day.

For instance, Steve Jobs was famous for starting each day with this question: "If today were the last day of my life, would I want to do what I am about to do today?"

What's your answer to that? What is your mission, vision or purpose? We already discovered that a true entrepreneur is not looking at money, but at the exit, the excitement created by building something that succeeds.

Unless you make a point of getting to know yourself, and make a habit of getting to know yourself again each day, you will be unable to choose the right habits to lead you to success.

Chapter Three

Intention

"Your net worth to the world is usually determined by what remains after your bad habits are subtracted from your good ones."

-Benjamin Franklin

Putting It All Together

Many experts will say that you just cannot teach entrepreneurship, but we now know just how wrong those experts can be.

Instead of looking at it through the filter of "teaching" it, we did something different in the previous chapters. We looked at it as different components (mindset and habits) and uncovered what you need to do, think and feel to be a success.

After all, anyone can learn things like accounting, marketing, finance and even some of the legalities of running a business or creating an enterprise. These are basic skills, but it is what one journalist described these as the "soft skills" of entrepreneurship, that are a bit more challenging.

She wrote: "when it comes to the hard skills, anyone can learn them...But, more important are the soft skills. These are trickier to learn. They don't come in a textbook or a webinar. They don't even necessarily come from working hard at your job. They come from inside you. you need to unlock them and foster them."

What are the soft skills considered in these pages? Just about everything!

Your mindset is not something that you learned from a book, it had been shaped by all of your previous life experiences. Though we went over some exercises you can use to re-train it, it is entirely in your hands whether you achieve this goal.

And those habits? These are also activities that you must foster, nurture and bring to their full fruition.

How do you put it all together?

Look back to the top of this page and you'll see that quote from Ben Franklin. He turned the answer into an equation - take away the habits that prevent you from succeeding and you have the habits that are worthy of fostering.

Yet, we also know that there is more to it.

Aligning Intention with Habits

Consider this idea about success. It is "largely determined by the extent you have a clear vision, habits and intentions set up."

So, your intentions can also be seen as your mindset and your habits are exactly as we have been considering. Your clear vision is something only you can map out, but we have already gone over all the steps and points you need to clarify that vision.

To be sure that you have it clear, though, let's do a quick series of questions to ensure your intention, vision and habits are aligned:

Who is it you aim to be?

How do you want to feel?

What is your purpose or goal?

What is it you wish to achieve or accomplish?

How is it you want those around you to feel?

Now, be very careful in answering these questions. If you don't have very clear answers to such questions, the world will answer them for you. In fact, the world might already be answering them for you.

For instance, if you have been operating in a fixed mindset, you might have spent years staying safe and comfortable in work you hate. You might answer the questions with replies that have nothing to do with your actual vision, nor the habits or intentions you wish to develop.

Instead, the world has answered those questions above for you, steering you towards behaviors or a mindset that is not productive or even functional. Now is the time to change that and turn your vision into your intention and habits. There are three clear ways to make it happen.

Instigating Change

Though you picked this up to learn the inner workings of the most successful entrepreneurs, you may now realize that it isn't just a laundry list of things you can do each day and "voila", you are a success.

Instead, it may be more about altering your mindset, creating new habits, developing different goals and relying on the details in these pages as you formulate actual plans.

In other words, to become like those successful entrepreneurs may mean making a lot of changes. The good news is that much of what you have already read has shown you exactly how to make the most effective changes. To be sure you do things in the most efficient way, though, let's consider a formulaic method for instigating major changes in mindset, habits and even your personal vision.

If you talk to behavioral experts and psychology professionals, most would tell you that there are three points to consider if you wish to make changes:

- *Decide*
- *Commit*
- *Act, and continue to act*

Deciding

We can't possibly know what issues you have decided to change, but we can say this, if you have decided to change, then make this a concrete thought in your mind. It must be positive and affirmative, and you must not reconsider the changes each time you realize your new pattern must be followed.

As one expert wrote, "You need to affirmatively make the decision and stop reconsidering it each time the circumstance arises. Do not re-analyze your decision as you will talk yourself out of it."

There cannot be a "Maybe I'll do it" or "Let's wait and see how I feel about that..." because you won't follow through.

A great example of deciding and following through is found in changing the time you get up each day. If you do not decide to do it, you will hit the snooze button, opt to rest "just a few more minutes".and guess what? You won't get up earlier.

So, instead of thinking about that change, decide that you are getting up at X hour and as soon as it ticks over to that hour, your feet should be hitting the floor.

You can enhance your ability to commit to decisions by visualizing the benefits, too. For instance, "if I get up at 5:30 each morning, I can get a full hour of.... done before work".

Keep deciding to get up at that time each day until your subconscious stops questioning it and it becomes a habit.

This decision process is also the same for changing your mindset and building new habits.

Committing

This is different than deciding, though it may not initially seem so. Committing is a lot like keeping your eye on the exit. This is because it is a process in which you are sticking with your decision until that process has reached whatever end is there. In other words, commit to that change and making it a habit.

It is about using the discipline, keeping that promise to yourself, knowing you'll regret not seeing it through, and accomplishing all you have chosen to do. It is much more than deciding, it is persisting, refusing to allow anything to get you off track, and being truer to yourself than ever before.

Acting.and Continuing to Act

They say that the proof is in the pudding, and it is true with this issue, too. You can keep deciding and even committing in your head, but once you act on your decisions and commitments, you are manifesting them into reality.

One of the simplest ways to see this brought to life is to decide to form a new habit. You decide on the habit, decide to develop it, commit to it, and then act. You must live that action every day, repeatedly committing and taking those steps to make it real.

You can only see change if you have persistently acted on the change you want to see.

You cannot wish for, hope or simply want change - it takes those three steps. These steps are also all that you need to bring your new mindset and habits to life and start striving towards your goals of being a successful entrepreneur.

Conclusion

Now you understand the difference between the traits that successful entrepreneurs share and the habits they share. You see that they are all unique and personal, and that habits are chosen by the entrepreneur (consciously or subconsciously) because they suit their needs and goals.

You also see that all of them have decided, committed to and acted on their vision - aligning their intention and habits with their goals. They are a persistent and impossible to beat group, and you can begin building or rebuilding yourself in their image today.

Never forget that growth mindset - it is the foundation of it all. You can be the best networker, the most creative problem solver, or the best at sales and marketing, but if you are not fueling your desire with the right mental energy, it could all be for nothing. After all, it is always your mindset that shapes your determination, behavior, initiative and perspective, and if it is telling you that you are not good enough or that your work is pointless - you will fail.

Don't let that happen. In these pages, you have been given all of the keys you need to alter your mindset, create new habits and really align all of your efforts and energies towards total success.

We'll close with a very potent quote from a business expert at Entrepreneur who had this to say about mindset: "before you invest your time, money and energy in developing a new strategy, or buying another blueprint, or hiring another coach or consultant, take a good look at what goes on in the space between your ears. Because that is where all the secrets to success really live, and where your strategy really lives or dies."

Sources

https://www.entrepreneur.com/article/243059

http://www.inc.com/jessica-stillman/the-one-belief-that-can-make-you-more- successful.html

https://www.forbes.com/sites/brettnelson/2012/06/05/the-real-definition-of-entrepreneur- and-why-it-matters/#73dff6ee4456

http://www.inc.com/jessica-stillman/8-ways-to-be-smarter.html

http://www.inc.com/jessica-stillman/3-beliefs-of-highly-successful-people.html

http://www.inc.com/jeff-haden/to-build-employee-performance-dont-praise-achievement- praise-effort.html

http://www.mindsetonline.com/whatisit/whatdoesthismeanforme/

https://www.entrepreneur.com/slideshow/248357

https://www.entrepreneur.com/article/289690

https://mic.com/articles/89579/science-shows-how-the-brains-of-intelligent-successful- people-are-different-from-everyone-else#.a0kKqdnOC

https://smallbiztrends.com/2016/05/habits-of-successful-entrepreneurs.html

https://medium.com/@Pcgmontgomery/mindset-habits-of-the-super-successful- entrepreneur-e13cf50e0dc0#.4q14axrmj

http://www.visualcapitalist.com/habits-highly-successful-entrepreneurs/

http://www.mindofwinner.com/4-habits-of-successful-entrepreneurs/

http://www.fortunebuilders.com/5-daily-habits-to-become-a-successful-entrepreneur/ https://www.psychologytoday.com/blog/hope-relationships/201605/the-power-positive- self-talk https://mic.com/articles/89579/science-shows-how-the-brains-of-intelligent-successful- people-are-different-from-everyone-else#.X6SvlVwws

https://www.entrepreneur.com/article/289690

http://www.fortunebuilders.com/5-daily-habits-to-become-a-successful-entrepreneur/

https://www.forbes.com/sites/groupthink/2013/02/13/what-drives-the-best-entrepreneurs-hint-its-not-money/#3eb1e2fa4348

https://renewingallthings.com/spiritual-health/how-to-make-life-changes-last-habit- intention/

https://www.entrepreneur.com/article/243643

www.ingramcontent.com/pod-product-compliance
Lightning Source LLC
Chambersburg PA
CBHW071119220526
45467CB00004B/1948